REBEL GiRLS EXPLORE

FRANCESCA CAVALLO
ELENA FAVILLI

20 TALES of EXTRAORDINARY WOMEN

Copyright © 2019 by Timbuktu Labs. All rights reserved. Published by Scholastic Inc., 557 Broadway, New York, NY 10012, by arrangement with Timbuktu Labs. SCHOLASTIC and all associated logos are trademarks and/or registered trademarks of Scholastic Inc.

Parts of this work have been previously published in the books *Good Night Stories for Rebel Girls* and *Good Night Stories for Rebel Girls 2*.

Created by Francesca Cavallo and Elena Favilli
Art Direction by Giulia Flamini
Graphic Design by Annalisa Ventura

ISBN: 978-1-338-56738-0

10 9 8 7 6 5 4 3 2 1   19 20 21 22 23

Printed in the U.S.A. 113

First Scholastic printing, September 2019

CONTENTS

PREFACE

Dearest Rebel,

In this book, you will explore the deepest trenches of the ocean with marine biologist Sylvia Earle, unearth dinosaur fossils with paleontologist Mary Anning, and soar beyond our planet with astronaut Mae Jemison. While these frontiers may seem to exist beyond your grasp, remember that they are well within reach. As you journey forward, new worlds will open up for you!

The women featured in this book mastered difficult subject matter from biology and computer science to chemistry and engineering, though they faced many obstacles on their way. These brave and intrepid explorers chose to ignore doubters and forge new paths.

We hope that their stories inspire you to embrace complex disciplines including science and math and ignore anyone who tells you that you can't. While these subjects may require hard work, practice, and perseverance, the joy of discovery is worth the hassle.

We can't wait to see what you will accomplish!

Dream bigger, aim higher, fight harder, and when in doubt, remember you are right.

Rebel Girls

AISHOLPAN NURGAIV

EAGLE HUNTRESS

Once there was a thirteen-year-old girl named Aisholpan who lived in the icy-cold Altai Mountains. For seven generations, the men in her tribe had hunted with golden eagles to provide their families with food and fur.

Golden eagles are big, fierce creatures with sharp claws and curved beaks that can be extremely dangerous. But to Aisholpan, they were simply beautiful. She longed to train an eagle of her own, so one day she said to her father, "Dad, I know that no girls have ever done this, but if you teach me, I'll be good." Her father, who was a great eagle hunter, paused to think.

Then he said, "You are strong. You are not afraid. You can do it."

Her heart sang with joy. Aisholpan and her dad rode their horses high into the snowy mountains. Finding an eaglet to train wasn't easy. Aisholpan reached a nest with a rope tied around her waist, trying not to slip on the sharp rocks. In the nest, she found a tiny golden eagle, all alone.

She covered the bird's head with a blanket to calm her down, then brought her home. Aisholpan sang and told stories so that the eaglet would recognize her voice. She fed her small chunks of meat and taught her how to land on her glove. "I treat her with respect, because if she trusts me, she won't fly away. We will be a team for a few years. Then I'll return her to the wild. The circle of life must continue."

Aisholpan became the first woman to enter the Golden Eagle competition in Ölgii, Mongolia. After her, three more girls started training to become eagle hunters.

BORN 2003

MONGOLIA

"PLAN TO TEACH
MY YOUNGER SISTER
EAGLE HUNTING."
AISHOLPAN NURGAIV

ILLUSTRATION BY
ALLY NIXON

AMELIA EARHART

AVIATOR

Once upon a time, a girl called Amelia saved enough money to buy a yellow airplane. She called it *The Canary*.

A few years later, she became the first woman to fly solo across the Atlantic Ocean. It was a dangerous flight. Her tiny plane was tossed around by strong winds and icy storms. She kept herself going with a can of tomato juice, sucked through a straw. After almost fifteen hours she touched down in a field in Northern Ireland, much to the surprise of the cows. "Have you come far?" the farmer asked her. "All the way from America!" she laughed.

Amelia loved to fly and she loved to do things no one had ever done before. Her biggest challenge was to be the first woman to fly around the world.

She could only take a small bag because all the space in the plane had to be used for fuel. Her long flight was going well. She was supposed to land on tiny Howland Island but never got there. In her last transmission, Amelia said she was flying through clouds and was running low on fuel. Her plane disappeared somewhere over the Pacific Ocean and was never found.

Before leaving, she wrote, "I am quite aware of the hazards. I want to do it because I want to do it. Women must try to do the same things that men have tried. If they fail, their failure must be a challenge to others."

JULY 24, 1897–CIRCA JULY 1937

UNITED STATES OF AMERICA

ILLUSTRATION BY
GIULIA FLAMINI

"ADVENTURE IS
WORTHWHILE IN ITSELF."
—AMELIA EARHART

JANE GOODALL

PRIMATOLOGIST

Once, in England, there was a girl called Jane who loved climbing trees and reading books. Her dream was to go to Africa and spend time with the wild animals there.

So, one day, Jane flew to Tanzania with her notebook and binoculars, determined to study real chimpanzees in their natural environment.

At first, it was hard to get close to them. The chimpanzees would run away the moment she was in sight. But Jane kept visiting the same place every day at the same time. Eventually, the chimps allowed her to get closer.

Getting closer was not enough for Jane: she wanted to become friends with them. So she started a "banana club." Whenever she visited the chimpanzees, she would share bananas with them.

At the time, little was known about chimpanzees. Some scientists used to observe them from far away, using binoculars. Others studied chimps in cages.

Jane, instead, spent hours hanging out with chimpanzees. She tried to speak to them using grunts and cries. She climbed trees and ate the same foods they ate. She discovered that chimpanzees have rituals, that they use tools, and that their language comprises at least twenty different sounds.

She even discovered that chimpanzees are not vegetarians.

Once, Jane rescued an injured chimpanzee and nursed it back to health. When she released it back into the wild, the chimpanzee turned and gave her a long, loving hug as if to say, "Thanks and bye!"

BORN APRIL 3, 1934

UNITED KINGDOM

ILLUSTRATION BY
EMMANUELLE WALKER

"ONLY IF WE UNDERSTAND, WILL
WE CARE. ONLY IF WE CARE,
WILL WE HELP. ONLY IF WE HELP,
SHALL ALL BE SAVED."
—JANE GOODALL

JESSICA WATSON

SAILOR

Once upon a time, there was a girl called Jessica who was afraid of water.

One summer morning, Jessica was playing with her sister and cousins by the pool. At one point, the other children lined up on the side, and got ready to jump in together holding hands.

Jessica's mom watched from the window to make sure Jessica was okay. She expected Jessica to step back from the edge, but was amazed to see her daughter step forward with the others. "One...two...three..." *Splash!* All the kids landed in the water, shouting and laughing.

From that day on, Jessica started loving the water. She joined a sailing club and decided to sail around the world on her own without stopping. She painted her boat bright pink and christened her, *Ella's Pink Lady*.

She packed the boat with steak and kidney pies, potatoes, cans and cans of beans, 150 bottles of milk, and lots of water, and set sail from Sydney Harbor. She was just sixteen years old.

All on her own, Jessica sailed onward. She fought against waves as tall as skyscrapers, she woke up to the most beautiful sunrises, spotted blue whales, and watched shooting stars above her boat.

Seven months later, she arrived back in Sydney. Thousands of people turned out to greet her. They rolled out a special carpet for her: bright pink, just like her boat!

BORN MAY 18, 1993

AUSTRALIA

"YOU CAN'T CHANGE
CONDITIONS—JUST
THE WAY YOU DEAL
WITH THEM."
—JESSICA WATSON

JOAN BEAUCHAMP PROCTER

ZOOLOGIST

One day, a girl called Joan asked her mom and dad to get her a pet. "I don't want a puppy or a kitten," she said. "I'd love a snake! And some lizards, please." By the time she was ten, Joan was looking after lots of reptiles. One of them, a large Dalmatian wall lizard, was her favorite; they traveled everywhere together, and even sat side by side at mealtimes. When she was older, Joan took her pet crocodile to school—much to the teacher's amazement!

These creatures fascinated Joan. She became a world expert in herpetology—the branch of zoology dealing with reptiles and amphibians—and got a job at the British Natural History Museum. Then one day, the London Zoo asked her to design a new reptile house. She did an excellent job and became something of a celebrity. Crowds gathered to watch her handling pythons, crocodiles, and huge Komodo dragons. She was named curator of reptiles.

A Komodo dragon named Sumbawa became Joan's special pet. Sumbawa followed her everywhere. Joan would stroke and pat her, and feed her chicken, pigeon, and eggs. Sometimes, she "steered" the dragon along by holding her tail. Joan understood these animals so well that she knew when they were sick, and exactly what to do to make them better.

Her own health problems, however, were harder to cure. She was constantly in pain, and had been for much of her life. But this didn't stop her from following her passion—even when it meant going to work in a wheelchair, with Sumbawa lumbering along happily behind her.

AUGUST 5, 1897–SEPTEMBER 20, 1931

UNITED KINGDOM

ILLUSTRATION BY
MARIJKE BUURLAGE

"WHY SHOULDN'T A WOMAN
RUN A REPTILE HOUSE?"
– JOAN BEAUCHAMP PROCTER

KATHERINE JOHNSON, DOROTHY VAUGHAN, AND MARY JACKSON

COMPUTER SCIENTISTS

Every day, Katherine, Dorothy, and Mary drove together to NASA, the agency responsible for the American space program. They were all brilliant scientists, and their job was to crack complex math problems to make sure that astronauts could travel safely to space.

When NASA bought its first IBM transistor-based computer, only a few people in the world knew how to use it for business—and no one knew how to use it for space travel! So Dorothy taught herself Fortran, the programming language the computer understood, and got the system working.

When astronaut John Glenn was about to take off for a trip orbiting the Earth, he said he did not completely trust the computer and asked Katherine to check the trajectory calculations herself. "If she says the numbers are good, I'm ready to go," he said.

When the opportunity to work on the Supersonic Pressure Tunnel came about, Mary volunteered. She specialized in the behavior of air around planes, and she became the first African American female aeronautical engineer.

Katherine, Dorothy, and Mary overcame incredible odds, but their contributions to science and technology remained unknown for many years. Today, they are celebrated as three of the most inspiring figures in the history of space travel.

KATHERINE JOHNSON, BORN AUGUST 26, 1918
DOROTHY VAUGHAN, SEPTEMBER 20, 1910–NOVEMBER 10, 2008
MARY JACKSON, APRIL 9, 1921–FEBRUARY 11, 2005
UNITED STATES OF AMERICA

ILLUSTRATION BY
CRISTINA PORTOLANO

"IN MATH, EITHER YOU'RE RIGHT
OR YOU'RE WRONG."
–KATHERINE JOHNSON

KATIA KRAFFT

Katia loved volcanoes. She didn't just like to look at pictures of boiling rivers of lava—she wanted to see them for real.

In college, Katia met a young man called Maurice who was as passionate about volcanoes as she was. On their first date, they realized they shared the dream of filming a volcano as it was erupting—something no one had ever done before. They fell madly in love and planned their first trip to an active volcano.

From then on, they were hooked. Whenever they heard that a volcano was about to blow, they packed their bags and rushed to the scene. To get the best shots, they would scramble up to the edge of the crater. They wore protective silver suits and helmets so they could withstand the heat from the molten lava—which was more than a thousand degrees.

Katia and Maurice's dream was to ride a boat down a lava flow! They knew their work was extremely dangerous, but they didn't care. To them, there was no sight more beautiful than a volcano erupting right before their eyes.

One day, Katia and Maurice were on the slopes of Mount Unzen, an active volcano in Japan. They were a safe distance from the summit— or so they thought. But this time, their calculations were wrong. The explosion was far larger than anyone had predicted, and it sent a boiling cloud of gases, rocks, and ash rolling down the valley. Katia, Maurice, and the members of their team had no chance to escape, and all tragically died.

APRIL 17, 1942 – JUNE 3, 1991

FRANCE

"VOLCANOES ARE SO POWERFUL, SO BEAUTIFUL, SO YOU CAN JUST FALL IN LOVE WITH THEM."
– KATIA KRAFFT

ILLUSTRATION BY MARTINA PAUKOVA

MAE C. JEMISON

ASTRONAUT AND DOCTOR

Once upon a time, there was a curious girl named Mae who could not make up her mind about what she wanted to be when she grew up.

Sewing dresses for her Barbie dolls, she wanted to be a fashion designer; reading a book about space travel, she wanted to be an astronaut; fixing a broken toy, she thought maybe an engineer would be better; going to the theater, she exclaimed, "Maybe I'll become a dancer."

The world was Mae's laboratory and she had plenty of experiments she wanted to try. She studied chemical engineering, African American studies, and medicine. She learned to speak Russian, Swahili, and Japanese. She became a doctor and volunteered in Cambodia and Sierra Leone. Then she applied to NASA to become an astronaut. Mae was selected and after one year of training, she was sent into space on board the space shuttle.

She carried out tests on the other members of the crew. Since she was not only an astronaut but also a doctor, her mission was to conduct experiments on things like weightlessness and motion sickness, which can be quite a problem when you're floating upside down in outer space.

When Mae came back to Earth, she realized that—while she had enjoyed space very much—her true passion was improving health in Africa. So she quit NASA and founded a company that uses satellites to do just that.

Mae Jemison was the first African American woman in space.

BORN OCTOBER 17, 1956
UNITED STATES OF AMERICA

"I ALWAYS KNEW I'D
GO TO SPACE."
—MAE C. JEMISON

MARIA REICHE

I n a small house in a Peruvian desert, there lived an adventurous German mathematician called Maria Reiche.

Etched into the dry desert rocks were hundreds of lines. No one knew what they were for, or why they were there, or even how old they were.

These mysterious lines, called Nazca Lines, became Maria's passion. She flew planes and helicopters to map the lines and—when there were no planes to fly—she just climbed the tallest ladder she could find to observe the lines from above. Some lines had been covered by dust so she used brooms to clean them. She used so many brooms that some people thought she was a witch!

As she studied the lines, she discovered something incredible. Those were not just random scratches: They were enormous drawings—made by the people who lived there thousands of years ago. There was a hummingbird! Intertwined hands! Flowers! A gigantic spider! All sorts of geometrical shapes!

Why would these ancient people create drawings that could only be seen from the sky? What were they? It was a mystery she was determined to solve.

She found that the lines corresponded to the constellations in the night sky. "It's like a giant map of the heavens," she said.

When Maria moved from Germany to Peru, she wasn't looking for giant mysterious drawings. But when she found them, she knew she would spend the rest of her life trying to figure them out. She became known as "The Lady of the Lines."

MAY 15, 1903–JUNE 8, 1998
GERMANY

"WHEN I FIRST CAME TO PERU
BY SEA, THE SHIP PASSED
THROUGH THE CENTER OF FOUR
CONSECUTIVE RAINBOWS: FOUR
ARCS, ONE INSIDE THE OTHER."
—MARIA REICHE

MARIA SIBYLLA MERIAN

NATURALIST

Maria was a little girl who loved art. Every day, she would gather flowers to paint. Sometimes, she found caterpillars on the flowers and made paintings of how they changed, day by day, into beautiful butterflies.

At that time, people believed that butterflies magically sprouted out of mud. Maria knew better, but no one believed her.

Years passed and Maria became a great watercolor artist. She wrote about her discoveries, but at the time scientists only took books in Latin seriously, and Maria's was in German.

One day, Maria and her daughter decided to move to a new city: Amsterdam. There, Maria found display cases filled with exotic insects collected from South America.

Maria thought, "If I could study these insects in their natural habitat, I could write a book that people would notice."

She sold her paintings and set sail for South America. In the rain forests of Suriname, Maria and her daughter climbed tall jungle trees to study the insects high up. Maria wrote her new book in Latin and this time, it was a huge success. Everybody learned that butterflies and moths come from caterpillars, not mud! The process is called metamorphosis (from the Greek word meaning to change shape). Today, we know that many animals metamorphosize: frogs, moths, beetles, crabs . . . and all thanks to the work of Maria Sibylla Merian!

APRIL 2, 1647–JANUARY 13, 1717
GERMANY

"IN MY YOUTH, I SPENT MY TIME
INVESTIGATING INSECTS."
—MARIA SIBYLLA MERIAN

MARY ANNING

PALEONTOLOGIST

In a tiny, cramped house on the south coast of England, there lived a girl called Mary. Her house was so close to the sea that sometimes the storms would flood it.

The winds and storms that swept along the coast often revealed fossils in the cliffs along the shoreline. These are the remains of prehistoric plants or animals that died a long time ago.

Mary could not go to school because her family was too poor, but she taught herself to read and write. She studied geology to learn more about rocks, and anatomy to learn more about the skeletons of the prehistoric animals she found.

One day, she saw a strange shape jutting out of a rock. Mary took out her special little hammer and carefully chipped away at the rock. Bit by bit, she uncovered a thirty-foot-long skeleton. It had a long beak, but it wasn't a bird. Rows of sharp teeth, but it wasn't a shark. Flippers, but it wasn't a fish. And a long thin tail! It was the first-ever discovery of that kind of dinosaur fossil, and she named it ichthyosaur, meaning fish-lizard.

At the time, people believed that Earth was only a few thousand years old. Mary's fossils helped prove that there had been life on our planet for hundreds of millions of years.

Scientists from all over the world came to see Mary, the self-taught scientist who loved walking by the sea.

MAY 21, 1799–MARCH 9, 1847

UNITED KINGDOM

NELLIE BLY

In a village in Pennsylvania, there was a girl who always dressed in pink. Her name was Nellie.

When her father died, the family fell on hard times, so she went out looking for a job to help her mom make ends meet.

One day, Nellie read an article in a local newspaper. It was called "What Girls Are Good For." In the article, girls who worked were described as "monsters," because the author believed that a woman's place was in the home. Furious, Nellie wrote a passionate letter to the editor.

Impressed by her writing style, the editor offered her a job as a reporter. Nellie soon proved to be a brave investigative journalist. She moved to New York and joined the *New York World*, a newspaper run by a famous man called Joseph Pulitzer. Once, she pretended to be mentally ill and got herself checked into a mental institution to expose how badly the patients were treated. She was fearless, clever, and compassionate.

The newspaper set her a challenge. Jules Verne had written a popular novel called *Around the World in Eighty Days*. Could she do it in less time? It took Nellie just a few hours to pack a small bag and set sail from New York on a steamer. Traveling by ship, rail, and even donkey, she set herself a grueling pace. People placed bets on whether she would succeed or fail. Finally, 72 days, 6 hours, and 11 minutes later, she arrived back in New York. She had made it!

MAY 5, 1864–JANUARY 27, 1922
UNITED STATES OF AMERICA

"I HAVE NEVER WRITTEN A WORD THAT DID NOT COME FROM MY HEART. I NEVER SHALL."
-NELLIE BLY

THE NEW

NELLIE BLY

BEST REPORTER IN THE U.S.

ILLUSTRATION BY ZARA PICKEN

POORNA MALAVATH

MOUNTAINEER

Once upon a time, a girl called Poorna went on a rock-climbing expedition with her classmates. When they arrived at Bhongir Rock, in southern India, she looked up at the huge cliff that she was supposed to climb. Her legs shook and there were tears in her eyes. "I'll never make it," she thought.

But Poorna's teacher, a local police officer, encouraged her. "You can do it," he said. So she tried. When she reached the top, she shouted for joy. "I'm not afraid of anything now," she said. "I can conquer Mount Everest!" And she wasn't just saying it—Poorna actually wanted to climb the highest mountain in the world.

Before setting off for that next adventure, she had to train hard. She built up her stamina playing kabaddi—a sport similar to a high-energy version of tag. She traveled to the high plateaus of northern India in the freezing winter, and she climbed to the top of Mount Renock, one of the most challenging peaks in the Himalayas.

When she was ready, she joined an expedition to scale Mount Everest. She wasn't at all afraid when she first saw the mighty mountain. "It's not that tall," she said to her coach. "We can do that in a day."

Well, it took fifty-two days to get to the top, but when she reached the summit, Poorna, age thirteen, became the youngest girl ever to make it.

Poorna went on to climb to the top of Mount Kilimanjaro, in Tanzania, but her highest aspiration is to become a police officer—just like the teacher who helped her conquer her fear.

BORN JUNE 10, 2000

INDIA

ILLUSTRATION BY
PRIYA KURIYAN

"I WANTED TO PROVE
THAT GIRLS CAN DO
ANYTHING."
– POORNA MALAVATH

RACHEL CARSON

ENVIRONMENTALIST

Once there was a girl who loved to write stories about animals. Her name was Rachel, and she would grow up to become one of the world's most passionate guardians of the environment.

After graduating university with a degree in zoology, Rachel went back home to care for her aging mother. She found a job writing a series of radio shows about fish. No one else could make marine biology sound so exciting, and Rachel's program, called *Romance Under the Waters*, was a big hit. It showed that she was not only an amazing scientist but also a fine writer.

Despite having to earn a living and care for her mother, Rachel found time to write two beautiful books, called *The Sea Around Us* and *The Edge of the Sea*. And when her sister died, she even adopted her two nieces, raising them as her own.

Years later, Rachel and her mother moved to a little town in the countryside. There she started to notice the impact of pesticides on wildlife. At that time, farmers routinely sprayed chemicals on their crops to protect them from insects. What Rachel discovered was that these chemicals were poisoning other plants, animals, birds, and even humans. She wrote a book about it called *Silent Spring*.

The people who sold pesticides tried to stop her, but Rachel kept on talking about what she'd learned. *Silent Spring* was voted one of the most important science books ever written. It has inspired millions of people to join the environmental movement and campaign for the well-being of all species on Earth, not just our own.

MAY 27, 1907–APRIL 14, 1964

UNITED STATES OF AMERICA

ILLUSTRATION BY SARAH WILKINS

"IN NATURE
NOTHING EXISTS ALONE."
– RACHEL CARSON

ROSALIND FRANKLIN

CHEMIST AND X-RAY CRYSTALLOGRAPHER

Once upon a time, there was a girl who discovered the secret of life. Her name was Rosalind, and she was an extraordinary chemist. She was also an X-ray crystallographer and worked as a researcher in the biophysics lab at King's College London.

Rosalind studied DNA, a molecule carrying information that tells our bodies how to develop and function. Today, we know that DNA is shaped like a double helix—basically a twisted ladder—but in Rosalind's time, the scientific community had no idea what DNA looked like.

Rosalind spent hundreds of hours using X-rays to photograph DNA fibers and trying to unveil the secret of life. She even improved the machines she used so she could get the best possible picture.

Each photo took about a hundred hours to develop. One day, her team got an incredible shot that provided groundbreaking information about the structure of DNA. They called it Photograph 51.

One of the scientists working with Rosalind, Maurice Wilkins, didn't like her, so without telling her, he sent the photo to two competing scientists who were also studying DNA. When those two scientists, James Watson and Francis Crick, saw the picture, their jaws dropped. They used Photograph 51 as the basis of their 3D model of DNA, which eventually won them the Nobel Prize in Physiology or Medicine.

Rosalind left King's College London to work in other areas. She made crucial discoveries about how viruses spread infection. For this—and for her vital contribution to the discovery of DNA—she is now acknowledged as one of the most important scientists of the twentieth century.

JULY 25, 1920–APRIL 16, 1958

UNITED KINGDOM

"SCIENCE AND EVERYDAY LIFE
CANNOT AND SHOULD NOT BE SEPARATED."
ROSALIND FRANKLIN

SAMANTHA CRISTOFORETTI

ASTRONAUT

Once upon a time, there was an engineer who brewed coffee in outer space. Her name was Samantha, and she was also an astronaut.

Samantha had studied mechanical engineering and aeronautics at university. After she graduated, she joined a flight school and finished at the top of her class. Samantha became a fighter pilot in the Italian Air Force, but she wanted to fly even higher.

So she applied to the European Space Agency to join its space program. Only six pilots out of more than eight thousand applicants were selected: Samantha was one of them.

For two years, she went through an incredibly hard training program. At an underwater military training camp in Houston, Texas, Samantha had to learn how to assemble equipment at the bottom of a pool four times deeper than a normal one, how to swim while wearing a space suit, and how to fight underwater. She even had to learn how to speak Russian!

Once she had mastered all that, she was ready to go.

At the International Space Station, Captain Cristoforetti performed over two hundred experiments to study how the human body reacts to long stretches of time spent in zero gravity. "In the future," she predicted, "the human race will live on multiple planets, so it's important to know what happens to our bodies in outer space."

During the mission, Samantha also experimented with different kinds of food. "Who would want to live on Mars," she asked, "if they could only eat stuff squeezed out of a tube?" She was the third European woman to travel to outer space—and the first person to brew coffee there!

BORN APRIL 26, 1977

ITALY

"ALWAYS REMEMBER, IF YOU HAVE TO CHOOSE BETWEEN AN EASY THING AND A HARD ONE, THE HARD ONE'S USUALLY A LOT MORE FUN."
– SAMANTHA CRISTOFORETTI

SARA SEAGER

Once upon a time, there lived a girl whose mind seemed to work much faster than anyone else's. She could make connections between things in the blink of an eye. She didn't watch TV because it seemed slow and boring. She preferred to be up in her bedroom looking through her telescope.

While other people looked at the Moon or the stars, Sara looked at the spaces in between. She knew that in the dark spaces, there were billions more stars, and that most of those had planets circling around them, just like the Earth orbits the Sun. Were they far enough from their own suns not to burn up? Were they near enough not to be permanently frozen? Were they in that sweet spot—that one chance in a million—where life could form?

Sara Seager grew up to be a real-life alien hunter. Her job at the Massachusetts Institute of Technology is to look for signs of life on exoplanets, which are planets beyond our own solar system that orbit stars in distant galaxies. In the hallway outside her office is a poster of one of them: a rocky desert with two suns burning in the sky, just like Luke Skywalker's home planet, Tatooine, in the *Star Wars* movies.

Sara is not very practical and admits she couldn't change a light bulb at home. But her two boys are proud of their mom—a certified genius, and one of the top astrophysicists in the world. She sometimes can't find their socks, but she just might find a whole new Earth!

BORN JULY 21, 1971

CANADA

"BEING A SCIENTIST
IS LIKE BEING
AN EXPLORER."
– SARA SEAGER

SYLVIA EARLE

MARINE BIOLOGIST

Once upon a time, there was a young scientist who loved to dive at night, when the ocean is dark, and you can't tell if the fish are asleep or awake.

"At night," she said, "you see lots of fish you don't see in the daytime." Her name was Sylvia.

Sylvia led a team of aquanauts: she and her team lived underwater for weeks, dived out of all kinds of underwater vehicles, and studied life in the ocean like no one before.

One night, Sylvia wore a special suit. White and gray, and as big as a space suit, it had a huge, domed helmet with four round windows to see out of. Six miles offshore, she dived deeper than anyone had ever been without a rescue tether. Down where the dark is blacker than the starless night, with only the feeble light of an underwater lamp, she put her foot on the ocean floor, just as the first man, in a similar costume but miles above her head, had put his footprint on the surface of the Moon.

"Without the ocean," she explained, "there would be no life on earth. No humans, no animals, no oxygen, no plants. If we don't know the ocean, we can't love it."

Sylvia has studied hidden currents, discovered underwater plants, and waved to deep-sea fish. "We must take care of the oceans," she says. "Will you join me in a mission to protect the Earth's blue heart?"

BORN AUGUST 30, 1935

UNITED STATES OF AMERICA

ILLUSTRATION BY
GERALDINE SY

"I'VE HAD THE JOY OF
SPENDING THOUSANDS OF
HOURS UNDER THE SEA. I
WISH I COULD TAKE PEOPLE
ALONG
TO SEE WHAT I SEE,
AND TO KNOW
WHAT I KNOW."
—SYLVIA EARLE

WANGARI MAATHAI

ACTIVIST

Once upon a time, in Kenya, there was a woman called Wangari who was born in Kenya, but left her home country to become the first women in East and Central Africa to earn a doctorate degree.

When she returned to Kenya, she dreamed of solving the environmental and unemployment concerns of the women in her region. You see, the lakes had started to dry up and streams had started to disappear near her village, Wangari knew she had to do something. She called a meeting with some of the other women.

"The government cut down trees to make room for farms, but now we need to walk for miles to collect firewood," one said.

"Let's bring the trees back," exclaimed Wangari.

"How many?" they asked.

"A few million should do it," she replied.

"A few million? Are you crazy? No nursery is big enough to grow that many!"

"We're not buying them from a nursery. We'll grow them ourselves at home."

So Wangari and her friends gathered seeds from the forest and planted them in cans. They watered and looked after them until the plants were about a foot tall. Then, they planted the saplings in their backyards.

It started with a few women. But, just like a tree sprouting from a tiny seed, the idea spread and grew into a widespread movement.

The Green Belt Movement expanded beyond Kenyan borders. Forty million trees were planted and Wangari Maathai was awarded the Nobel Peace Prize for her work. She celebrated by planting a tree.

APRIL 1, 1940–SEPTEMBER 25, 2011

KENYA

ILLUSTRATION BY
THANDIWE TSHABALALA

"THE TIME IS NOW."
—WANGARI MAATHAI

ZHENYI WANG

ASTRONOMER

O nce upon a time, in China, there was a young girl who liked to study all sorts of things. She loved math, science, geography, medicine, and writing poetry. She was also great at horse riding, archery, and martial arts. Her name was Zhenyi.

Zhenyi traveled widely and was curious about everything but above all, she loved astronomy. She spent hours studying the planets, the Sun, the stars, and the Moon.

At that time, people thought that a lunar eclipse was a sign that the gods were angry. Zhenyi knew this couldn't be true and decided to prove it with an experiment. She put a round table—the Earth—in a garden pavilion, and from the ceiling she hung a lamp—the Sun. Off to one side, she placed a big round mirror—the Moon.

Then she started to move these objects exactly as they move in the sky until the Sun, Earth, and Moon stood in a line, with the Earth in the middle. "There you go! A lunar eclipse happens every time the Moon passes directly through the Earth's shadow."

Zhenyi also understood the importance of making math and science accessible for common people, so she got rid of all the aristocratic language and wrote a paper explaining the force of gravity.

Her reputation spread far and wide. In her poems, she often wrote about the importance of equality between men and women.

1768–1797

CHINA

"DAUGHTERS CAN ALSO BE HEROIC."
— ZHENYI WANG
ILLUSTRATION BY ANA GALVAÑ
ANAGALVAÑ

WRITE YOUR STORY

DRAW YOUR PORTRAIT

WHAT KIND OF EXPLORER ARE YOU?

If you have a burning curiosity to learn something new or go where no one has gone before, YOU are an explorer. Take this quiz to find out what kind of explorer you are!

1. WHERE IS YOUR FAVORITE PLACE TO GO EXPLORING?

A. My secret lab
B. Anywhere outside in nature
C. Above the clouds!

2. WHAT OBJECTS DO YOU ALWAYS CARRY WITH YOU?

A. Lab tools (thermometer, test tubes, magnifier)
B. Survival kit (water bottle, note pad, compass)
C. Adventure gear (parachute, telescope, star chart)

3. WHAT DESCRIPTION SOUNDS MOST LIKE YOU?

A. I'm focused, clever, and a little anti-social.
B. I'm spunky, curious, and cheerful.
C. I'm brave, fearless, and determined.

4. WHAT'S YOUR FAVORITE LIVING THING TO STUDY?

A. Anything teeny-tiny. Single-cell organisms are fascinating!
B. I can't choose! Plant or animal? Bird, amphibian, or fish?!
C. Aliens! Earthlings can't be the ONLY living beings.

5. WHEN SOMEONE TELLS YOU IT CAN'T BE DONE, YOU . . .

A. Hand over a report complete with data, formulas, and graphs.
B. Ignore them.
C. Do it anyway, better than anyone has done before.

6. WHICH INCREDIBLE INVENTION HAS "YOU" WRITTEN ALL OVER IT?

    A. Mathematics Doggo-bot—a robotic puppy that can do math.
    B. DJ Enviro-Clean 5000—a pollutant vacuum for sky, water, and land that also blasts my favorite songs.
    C. The Wizz-o-matic Flying Engine—it can make ANYTHING fly.

7. WHAT'S YOUR FAVORITE FOOD?

    A. Something I cooked up myself
    B. Vegan trail mix and kale chips
    C. Astronaut ice cream

8. WHAT IS YOUR FAVORITE THING TO STUDY?

    A. Fire and other chemical reactions
    B. Fossils or rock formations
    C. Asteroids, planets, and stars

9. IF YOU COULD BE ANY ANIMAL, WHICH ONE WOULD IT BE?

    A. An elephant—then I wouldn't have to memorize my notes.
    B. An extinct species, so I can see it in real life. Maybe a dinosaur!
    C. A bird, so I can see the world from the sky.

10. IF THE WORLD WAS ABOUT TO END, WHAT WOULD YOU BE DOING?

    A. Inventing something to avoid the apocalypse
    B. Finding the most fertile soil to grow food
    C. Venturing into space to search for a new habitable planet

Check out your results on page 45!

ANSWERS TO
"WHAT KIND OF EXPLORER ARE YOU?"

MOSTLY A'S

You're the Lab Rat! You love fiddling with all marvels modern technology has to offer. Test tubes! Beakers! Metal tables! Dangerous chemicals! Robots! Eh, so it might be a little "explosive." But this is the kind of discovery you were MADE for.

MOSTLY B'S

You're the Mapless Maverick! You trek up mountains and volcanoes, get lost in the wilderness for days, and climb jungle trees as well as the chimps themselves. Whether it be oceans, insects, or lava, you know there's a lot of beauty out there and you want to see all of it!

MOSTLY C'S

You're the Sky Warrior! Whether by plane, spaceship, or hang glider, you love to explore the open air and defy the mundane ties of gravity. You might spend your days staring at cloud shapes and your nights looking out at the stars wondering what else is out there.

EXPLORERS Q&A

Read about the curiosity of authors Elena and Francesca and how they created their books.

WHAT WAS IT LIKE EMIGRATING FROM ITALY?

It was exciting and hard. We were really lucky to have friends in California who opened their houses to us and hosted us first in Berkeley and then in San Francisco. Without their help, it would have been even harder. The U.S. and Italy are two very different countries, and it takes a lot of energy to get used to new languages, new food, new places, and new people who grew up differently than you. We recommend that you try spending a year in another country during your lifetime. It can change your life and open your mind to all sorts of new possibilities.

DO YOU SEE YOURSELVES AS EXPLORERS?

Absolutely yes! We moved far away from home to explore another country, we explored an industry we had never worked in before, and we explored new ways of making stories. It has been and continues to be an incredibly exciting journey.

WHAT WAS THE HARDEST THING ABOUT WRITING A BOOK?

First, deciding what to write about, and then figuring out how to write about it. For example, we had to decide how long the stories would be, how they would start, and what format they would take. We tried to write the stories in several formats until we found the one that felt just right. We decided on fairy tales and bedtime stories, so it felt right to begin many of the stories with "Once upon a time..."

INTERVIEW WITH THE AUTHORS

HOW DO YOU COME UP WITH IDEAS?

The books we write and the projects we create come from talking about things we like (and things we don't!). We are both very passionate about politics and art, so these are topics we talk about. Sometimes specific ideas emerge out of these conversations, like *Goodnight Stories for Rebel Girls*. We try not to fall in love with our ideas, so we test them, analyze them, and discuss them with our team. Only truly exceptional ideas are brought to life.

HOW LONG DID IT TAKE YOU TO CREATE YOUR BOOKS AND HOW DID YOU DO IT?

It took a whole year! We researched and wrote furiously. Then we sent the stories to the artists to illustrate the portraits of each woman. Our design team set the text and art into a layout, and then our editors got to work checking the facts and looking for mistakes. We sent the book to the printer after that, but our work wasn't done yet! We spread the word about our book by talking about it to newspapers and everyone we met, posting on social media, and sending out email newsletters. Then we finally got to hold our book in our hands.

HOW DID YOU CHOOSE THE WOMEN TO INCLUDE IN YOUR BOOKS?

We wanted to write about women from as many countries and backgrounds as possible to show the diversity of rebel girls all over the world. We also wanted to show the variety of women's careers: trombonists, marine biologists, judges, presidents, spies, chefs, surfers, poets, and rock singers. Finally, we selected women whose personal stories had a special surprising twist, like the fact that the famous chef, Julia Child, started her career as a spy cooking shark-repellent cakes during World War II.

WHAT DO YOU WANT READERS TO KNOW AFTER THEY'VE READ YOUR BOOKS?

That girls can do and be anything they want. Girls have the right to explore wildly, be ambitious, make mistakes, and discover extraordinary things. As Zhenyi Wang said, "Daughters can also be heroic."

CARING FOR THE EARTH

The natural world is a fascinating place! Spending time in nature lets you appreciate the air we breathe that is made by plants, the food we eat that grows, the water we drink from rivers and streams, the plant medicine that heals us, and the beauty surrounding all of it. Try the activities below to practice spending more time in nature and giving back to the world that gives us life!

EXERCISE 1:

Actions like Wangari Maathai's (page 37) effort to grow trees out of cans shows that you don't need much to be a steward (a person who looks after something or someone) of the environment. Try this activity at home!

1. Gather your materials:

   - A recycled can
   - A saucer to catch the drainage, like a plastic lid or dish
   - Soil
   - Seeds
   - Spray bottle
   - Plastic wrap

2. Fill three-quarters of your can with soil.
3. Follow the instructions on the seed packet for planting depth.
4. Cover the hole with soil and water, and cover with plastic wrap to keep in the moisture.
5. Place your potted plant on the saucer, by a window, and watch over the coming days and weeks as your plant grows! Don't forget to check the soil and water when needed.

EXERCISE 2:

Have you ever taken time to slowly observe the natural world around you? Maria Sibylla Merian (page 19) discovered metamorphosis because she spent time quietly studying butterflies.

1. Gather a blank notebook and a pencil.
2. Set up a comfortable spot in a natural place that you really enjoy.
3. Focus on one area that looks interesting to you.
4. Record what you have observed today—you can draw what you see, write notes, or a combination of both!

EXERCISE 3:

Write an inspiring story about explorers like Jane Goodall (page 5) or Joan Beauchamp Procter (page 9). Follow these instructions to help you write your story:

1. First, research different endangered animals. Choose your favorite and find out where they live, why they are endangered, and what people or organizations are doing to help them. Maybe you have even visited an endangered animal before at a zoo, nature preserve, or in the wild.

2. Explain how you met your animal friend. Describe your travels to where your friend lives, describe the habitat it lives in, what it eats, and how it behaves.

_____

_____

_____

3. How are you and your animal friend similar? How are you different?

_____

_____

_____

ILLUSTRATORS

Nineteen extraordinary female artists from all over the world illustrated the portraits in this book. Here are their names!

MARIJKE BUURLAGE, **NETHERLANDS**, 10

JOANA ESTRELA, **PORTUGAL**, 34

GIULIA FLAMINI, **ITALY**, 4

ANA GALVAÑ, **SPAIN**, 40

AMANDA HALL, **USA**, 20

KATHRIN HONESTA, **INDONESIA**, 8

PRIYA KURIYAN, **INDIA**, 26

LIEKELAND, **NETHERLANDS**, 30

KARABO MOLETSANE, **SOUTH AFRICA**, 16

SALLY NIXON, **USA**, 2

MARTINA PAUKOVA, **SLOVAKIA**, 14, 22

ZARA PICKEN, **USA**, 24

CRISTINA PORTOLANO, **ITALY**, 12

GAIA STELLA, **ITALY**, 18

GERALDINE SY, **PHILIPPINES**, 36

GIULIA TOMAI, **ITALY**, 32

THANDIWE TSHABALALA, **SOUTH AFRICA**, 38

EMMANUELLE WALKER, **CANADA**, 6

SARAH WILKINS, **NEW ZEALAND**, 28

ABOUT THE AUTHORS

Elena Favilli and Francesca Cavallo grew up in Italy. They are *New York Times* best-selling authors whose work has been translated into more than forty-five languages, and they have written for and been reviewed in various publications, including the *Guardian, Vogue,* the *New York Times*, *El País*, the *Los Angeles Times*, *Colors Magazine*, *Corriere della Sera*, and *La Repubblica*. They are the founders of Timbuktu Labs, and they live in Venice, California.

Timbuktu Labs is an award-winning media company founded in 2012 by Elena Favilli and Francesca Cavallo. Through a combination of thought-provoking content, stellar design, and business innovation, Timbuktu is redefining the boundaries of indie publishing to inspire a global community of progressive families spanning seventy countries. Timbuktu is home to a diverse and passionate group of rebels who work together in Los Angeles, New York, Atlanta, Mérida (Mexico), London, and Milan.